MW01701843

AUNTY V'S BOOKS

PENMANSHIP PERFECT!

Beginners Level

WORKBOOK 1

STRAIGHT EDITION

Veronica Carasquero

Penmanship Perfect! - Straight Edition

ISBN: 978-976-96941-2-5

Author & Creator: Veronica Carasquero, Maria Montessori Dip.Ed, B.Ed. & M.Ed.

Editors: Veronica Carasquero, Zara Mongru & Renee Simeon

Cover/Interior Design: Renee M. Simeon, OTWP Publishing
www.offthewheatenpathtt.com/OTWPublishing

Table of Contents

This book belongs to:

My name is

I am years old

I attend

school.

Preface

This book is suitable for Pre-Schoolers and Primary school students.

Welcome to the pleasant and rewarding journey of penmanship. Handwriting needs to begin early in order to have comprehensive and recognizable legibility of hand-written scripts. The formation in the early stages of life is important, as this is the pattern/s the children will hold on to or be most comfortable with for the rest of their life. This is why it is of great importance to teach the proper formation of the letters in the early years.

Another factor that is important is, the parent/ guardian/ care giver/teacher and so forth, read the instructions, practice the formations beforehand and be prepared to teach. Preparation includes; providing a comfortable table and chair, ensuring the child is not tired, has eaten and drank something, used the bathroom, washed their hands and is comfortable and ready to write.

The stationeries and book needed are:

- √ Two sharpened pencils- (the reason being when the point has broken another can be given therefore time and concentration is not lost.)
- √ A sharpener with a catchment or if this is not available the use of a regular sharpener can be used ensuring that a bin is close by to dispose of the shavings immediately.
- √ An eraser, apart from the one on the pencil.
- √ The Penmanship Perfect! penmanship book off course.

What is of utmost importance is undivided attention and supervision. Failure to supervise the child will defeat the objective that is supposed to be achieved. Please ensure that the person who is monitoring this activity is in no way distracted. The unsupervised child will quickly practice the wrong formation. Bad habits catch on quickly! Please do not let the child fall prey to this.

Formulating a daily routine and consistency is the key to success in anything you do. Therefore, this disposition should be engendered.

Please peruse the samples in the *Penmanship Perfect!* penmanship book to envision what can be achieved. The adult and the child after having done the first exercise would notice there is a consistent structure of writing. Thereafter, the large or small red and blue lined exercise book facilitates more needed practice, please continue the same structure from the workbook. Only one page per letter may be necessary while writing in the red and blue lined exercise book. However, children learn at different rates, therefore, additional practice can be given to engage the children in further practice.

Important:

The structure of this book facilitates the learning of mainly manuscript, common and capital letters formation. This skill will allow them to write words such as; their name, days of the week, the months of the year, subjects, in addition, sentences and any other form of written information. This skill will also enable the child to head up in their exercise book at school and be able to record work from off the board. This will indeed make it easier for everyone especially teachers. Most of all legible writing will be achieved.

As the saying goes give a fisherman a fish and you will have to feed him for life but show a fisherman to fish and you have taught him a skill forever.

In other words, do not write for the children or let them do what they want but rather teach them that much needed lifelong skill properly, so that they can hold on to it forever!

The pictures in this book promotes reinforcing the letter sounds. They were well thought out by the author as to stimulate the child's creative mind to imagine beyond what the picture is about. Please read the "Fun Facts" or Foot Notes" to guide the process of curiosity.

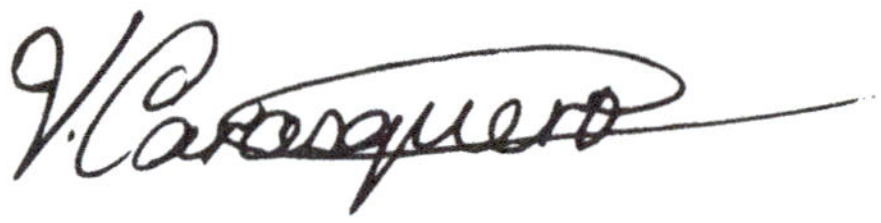

Tips for teaching left handers to write

SITTING POSITION

√ Ensure the child's feet is flat on the ground and not off the ground.

√ When the child arms are at his side, the height of the table should be 5cm above his/her elbow.

LETTER FORMATION

√ It is advised that left handers should cross their "f & t" from right to left. This helps with fluency in writing.

DESK POSITION

√ Please be advised do not place a left hander and right hander next to each other. (Their elbows will be bouncing each other)

PAPER POSITION

√ The page or book should be in line with the child's midline, then tilted 30 degrees clockwise (leaning slightly to the left) for a smooth flow of writing.

FINGER POSITION OF THE PENCIL

√ Hold the pencil 2.5 cm from the tip, a sticker can be placed on the pencil as a reminder to the lefthander where to position his/her fingers.

COPYNG LETTERS AND NUMBERS

√ The BOOK or WORKSHEET should be placed on the right side so as not to block him/her from copying.

How to use this book

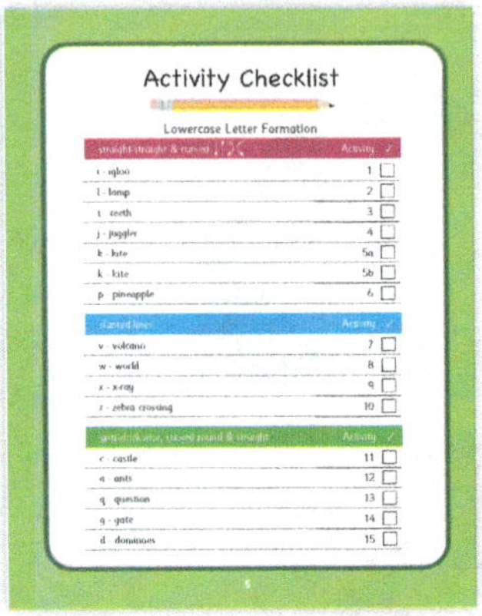

Activity Checklist:

√ Use this section to check off completed activities.

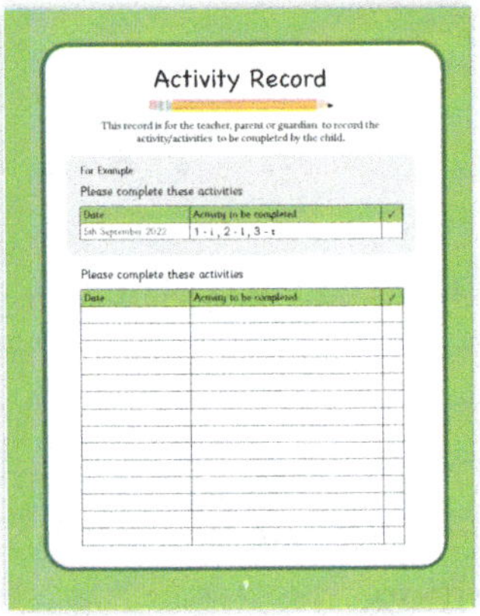

Activity Record:

√ Use this section assign activities.

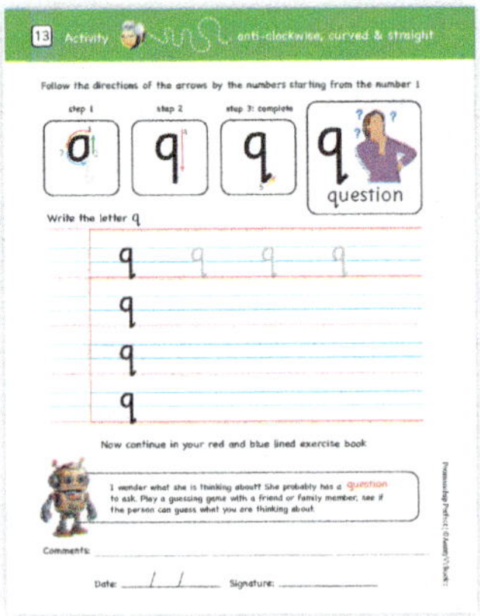

Sample Page:

√ This is a sample of what each page looks like.

Sample Page - Lowercase

13 Activity  anti-clockwise, curved & straight

Follow the directions of the arrows by the numbers starting from the number 1

step 1 | step 2 | step 3: complete

Write the letter q

q q q q
q
q
q

Now continue in your red and blue lined exercise book

I wonder what she is thinking about? She probably has a question to ask. Play a guessing game with a friend or family member, see if the person can guess what you are thinking about.

Comments: ______________________

Date: ____/____/____ Signature: ______________

Sample Page - Uppercase

STRAIGHT & ACROSS ACTIVITY 29

Follow the directions of the arrows by the numbers starting from the number 1

step 1 step 2 step 3: complete

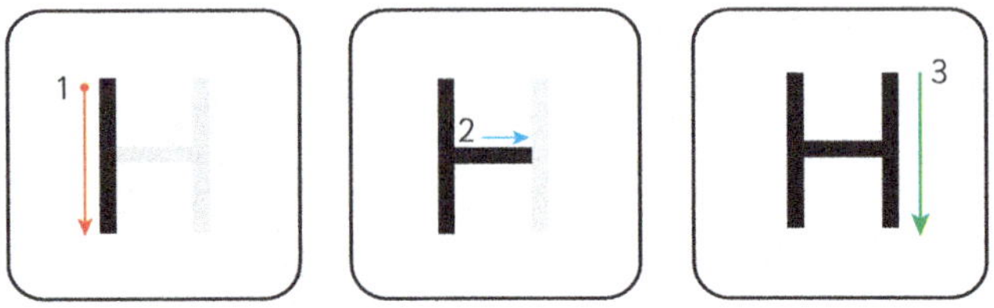

H 

HEDGEHOG

Write the letter H

H H H H

H

H

H

Now continue in your red and blue lined exercise book

Fun Fact: Did you know that HEDGEHOGS love to explore mazes and tunnels? Do a HEDGEHOG craft this week.

Comments: ______

Date: ___/___/___ Signature: ______

Activity Checklist

Lowercase Letter Formation

straight-straight & curved	Activity	✓
i - igloo	1	☐
l - lamp	2	☐
t - teeth	3	☐
j - juggler	4	☐
k - kite	5	☐
p - pineapple	6	☐

slanted & across	Activity	✓
v - volcano	7	☐
w - world	8	☐
x - x-ray	9	☐
z - zebra crossing	10	☐

anti-clockwise, curved & straight	Activity	✓
c - castle	11	☐
a - ants	12	☐
q - question	13	☐
g - gate	14	☐
d - dominoes	15	☐

straight, curved & clockwise	Activity	✓
r - rainbow	16	☐
n - net	17	☐
h - house	18	☐
m - map	19	☐
b - ball	20	☐

odd-different lines	Activity	✓
s - salamander	21	☐
f - flag	22	☐
u - underwater	23	☐
y - yoga	24	☐

stand alone	Activity	✓
o - otter	25	☐
e - eggs	26	☐

UPPERCASE LETTER FORMAtION

Activity Record

This record is for the teacher, parent or guardian to record the activity/activities to be completed by the child.

For Example:

Please complete these activities

Date	Activity to be completed	✓
8th May 2023	Pg1 - letter/s i, l	

Please complete these activities

Date	Activity to be completed	✓

Date	Activity to be completed	✓

Date	Activity to be completed	✓

Congratulations! You Did It!

Pre-writing Activities

Patterns for Penmanship Perfect!

Start at the green dot end at the red dot until you reach the Robot.

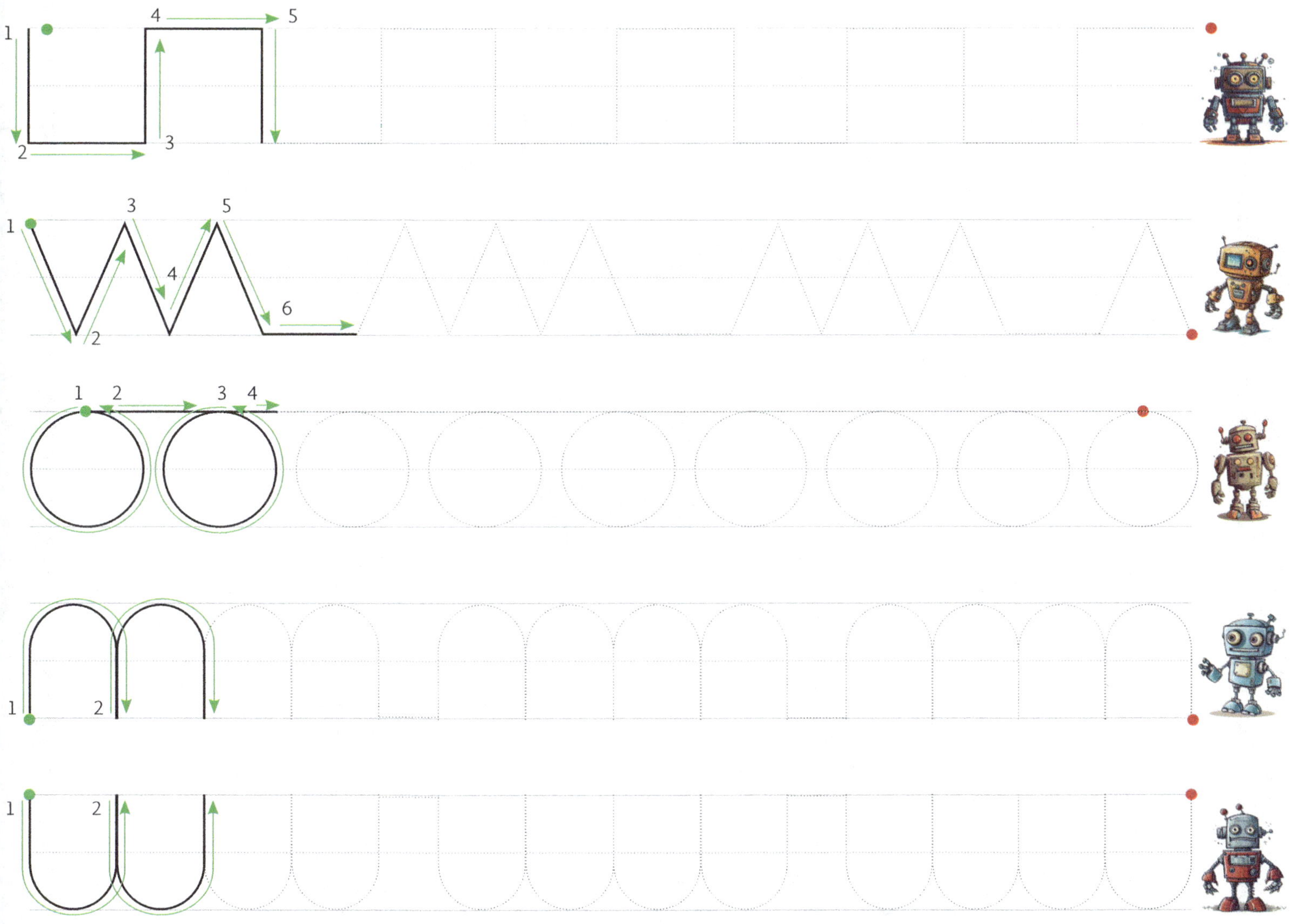

You made the robot happy by completing all the lines!

Comments: ____________________

Date: ____/____/____ Signature: ____________________

Lowercase Letters

a b c d e f g h i j k l m

n o p q r s t u v w x y z

Lowercase Letter Formation Grouped

straight-straight & curved

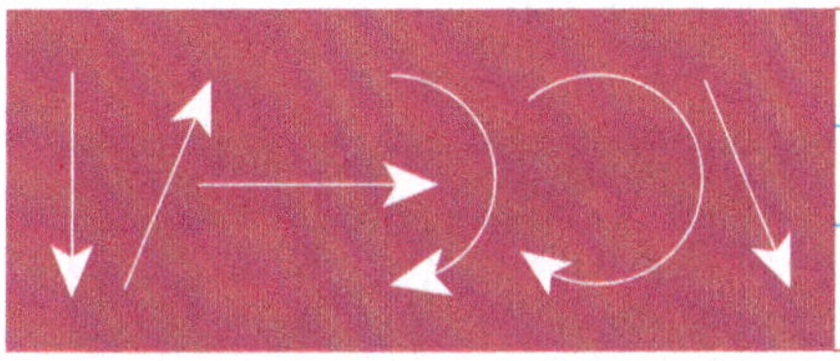

i l t j k p

slanted & across

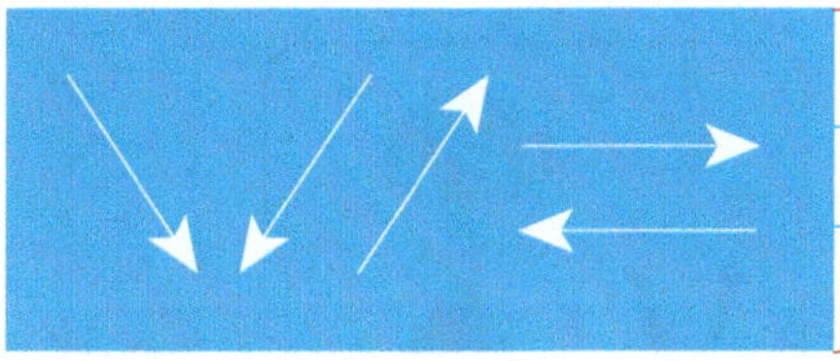

v w x z

anti-clockwise, curved & straight

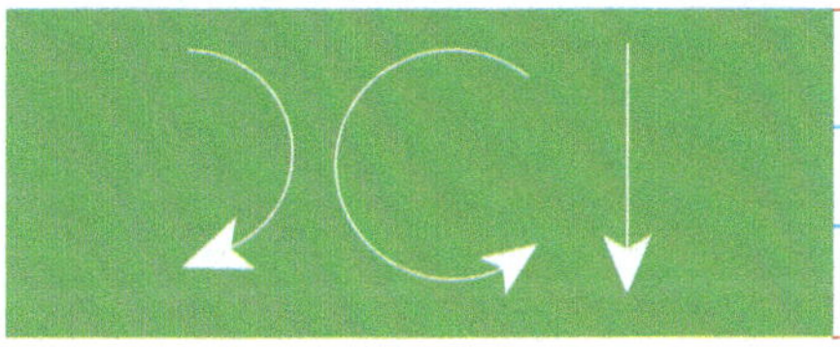

c a q g d

straight, curved & clockwise

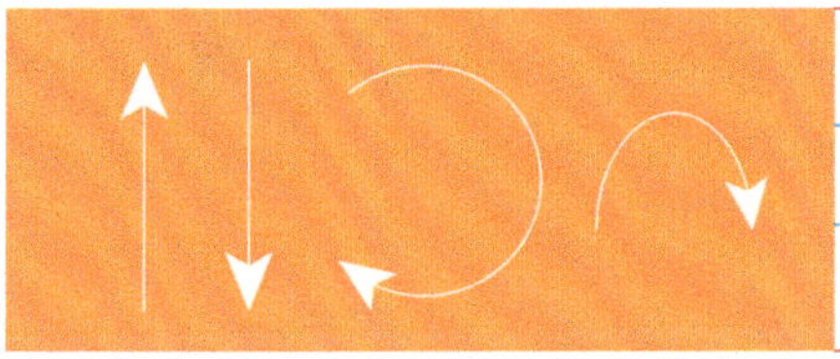

r n h m b

odd & different lines

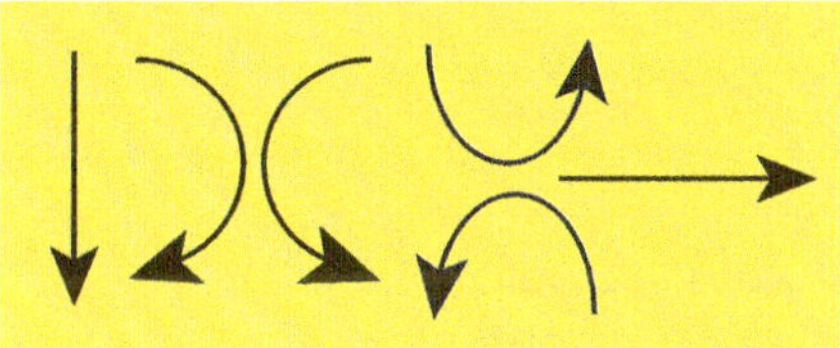

s f u y

stand alone, rounded & straight

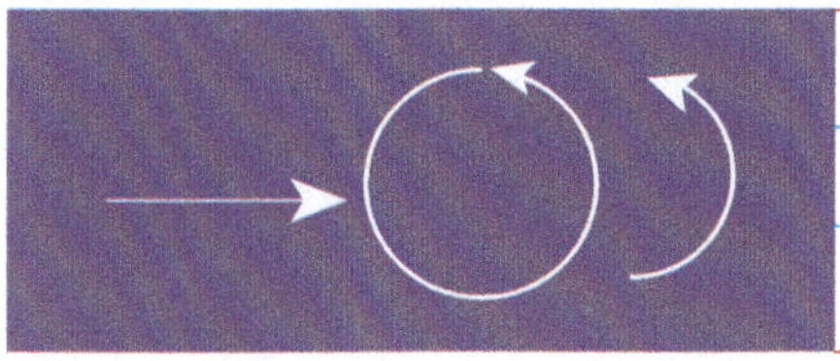

o e

Sample Page

All the letters should be completed like this in three rows for all the activities.

slanted & across  Activity 7

Follow the directions of the arrows by the numbers starting from the number 1

step 1	step 2	step 3: complete	
1 \	1 \/ 2	V 3	V volcano

Write the letter V

V V V V

V

V

V

Now continue in your red and blue lined exercise book

With the assistance of an adult, make a functional model of a volcano. Materials you can use for the lava liquid: flour, baking soda, vinegar, food colouring and water.

Comments: ______________________

Date: ____/____/____ Signature: ______________

straight, straight & curved

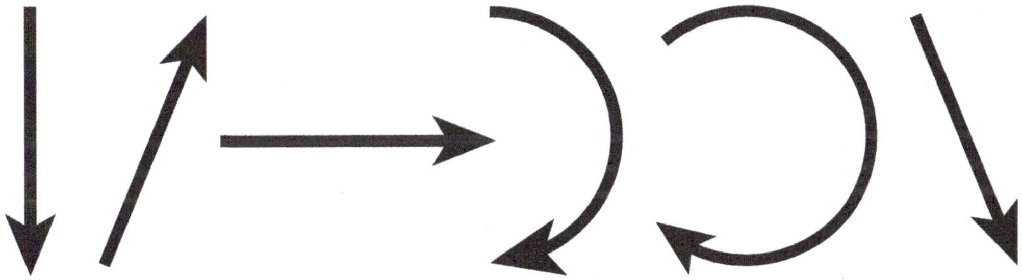

i l t j k p

Follow the directions of the arrows by the numbers starting from the number 1

step 1

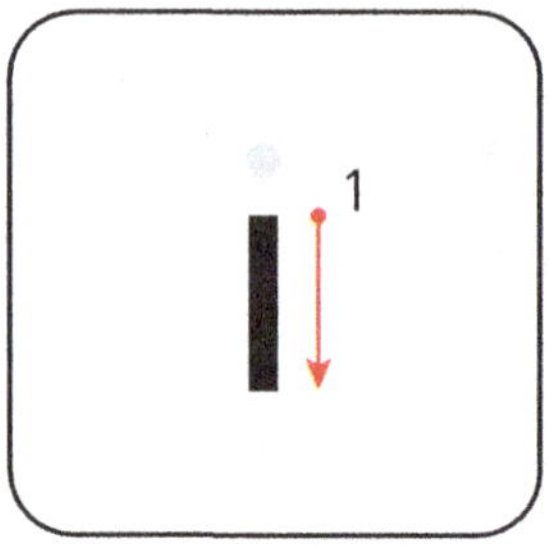

step 2

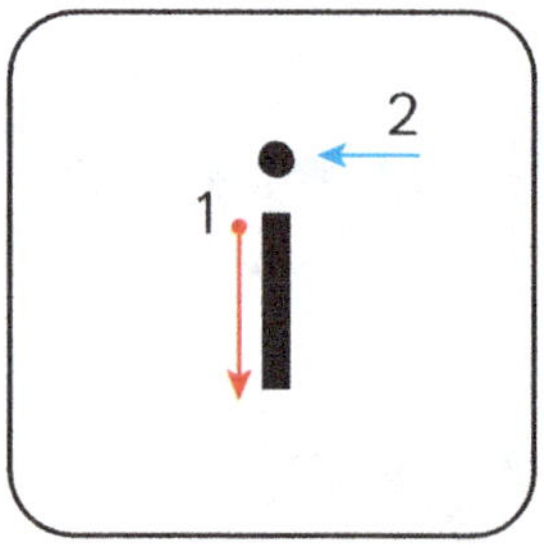

step 3: complete

i 

igloo

Write the letter i

i i i i

i

i

i

Now continue in your red and blue lined exercise book

Do you know that Eskimos live in igloos. Do some research to see how they live and also explore other types of houses people live in.

Comments: ____________________

Date: ___/___/___ Signature: ____________________

Follow the directions of the arrows by the numbers starting from the number 1

step 1	step 2	step 3: complete
1 l	1 l	l

l 
lamp

Write the letter l

l

l

l

l

Now continue in your red and blue lined exercise book

Remember to conserve energy by unplugging the lamp when it is not in use.

Comments:

Date: / /

Signature:

Follow the directions of the arrows by the numbers starting from the number 1

step 1

1

step 2

2

step 3: complete

t

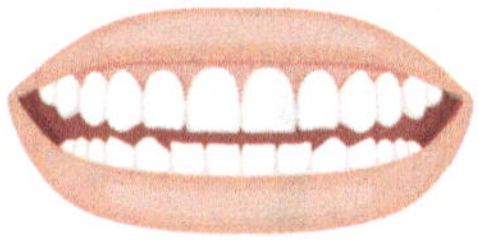

t teeth

Write the letter t

t

t

t

t

Now continue in your red and blue lined exercise book

Remember to brush your teeth three times a day and visit the dentist regularly.

Comments:

Date: / /

Signature:

Follow the directions of the arrows by the numbers starting from the number 1

step 1

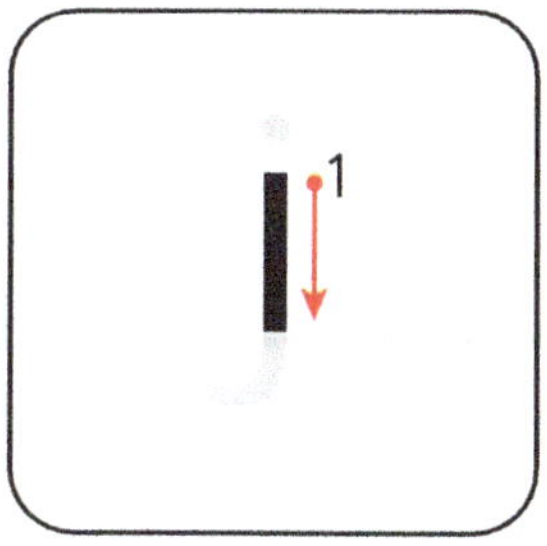

step 2

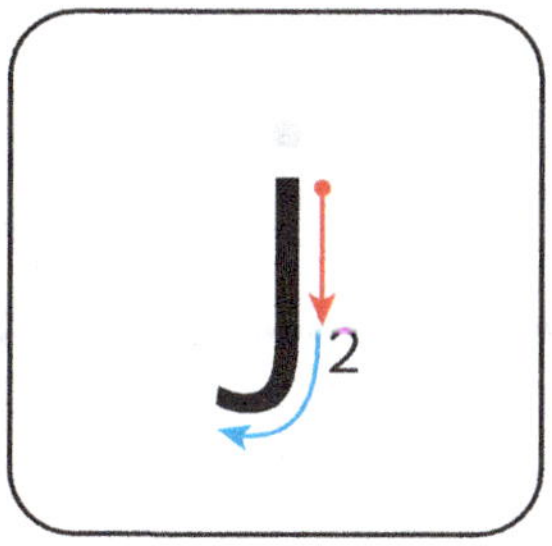

step 3: complete

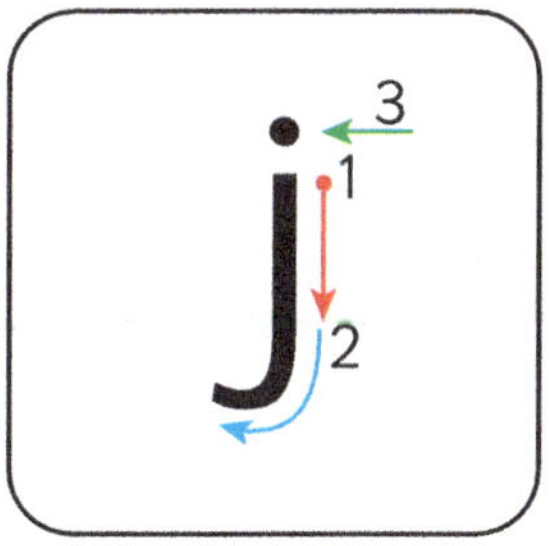

j

juggler

Write the letter j

j j j j
j
j
j

Now continue in your red and blue lined exercise book

Ask your parents or guardian to show you how to juggle like the juggler.

Comments: ____________________

Date: ____/____/____ Signature: ____________________

Follow the directions of the arrows by the numbers starting from the number 1

step 1 step 2 step 3: complete

Write the letter k

k k k k

k

k

k

Now continue in your red and blue lined exercise book

Try to make a kite or purchase one, then share that moment of flying a kite on the weekend.

Comments:

Date: / / Signature:

Follow the directions of the arrows by the numbers starting from the number 1

step 1	step 2	step 3: complete
1 l	1 2 r	1 2 3 p

p

pineapple

Write the letter p

p p p p
p
p
p

Now continue in your red and blue lined exercise book

Do you know that pineapples contain disease fighting antioxidants?
Make some pineapple chow today!

Comments: ____________________

Date: ___/___/___ Signature: ____________________

slanted lines

v w x z

Follow the directions of the arrows by the numbers starting from the number 1

step 1 | step 2 | step 3: complete

V volcano

Write the letter V

V V V V

V

V

V

Now continue in your red and blue lined exercise book

With the assistance of an adult, make a functional model of a volcano. Materials you can use for the lava liquid: flour, baking soda, vinegar, food colouring and water.

Comments: ____________________

Date: ___/___/___ Signature: ____________________

Follow the directions of the arrows by the numbers starting from the number 1

step 1

step 2

step 3: complete

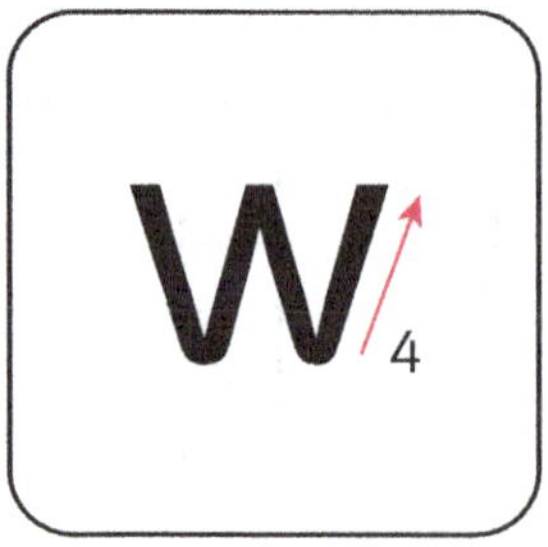

W

world

Write the letter W

W W W W

W

W

W

Now continue in your red and blue lined exercise book

The world is in our hands....please take care of it by recycling and planting a plant.

Comments: ______________________

Date: ___/___/___ Signature: ______________

Follow the directions of the arrows by the numbers starting from the number 1

step 1	step 2	step 3: complete
1 \	X 2	X 2

X 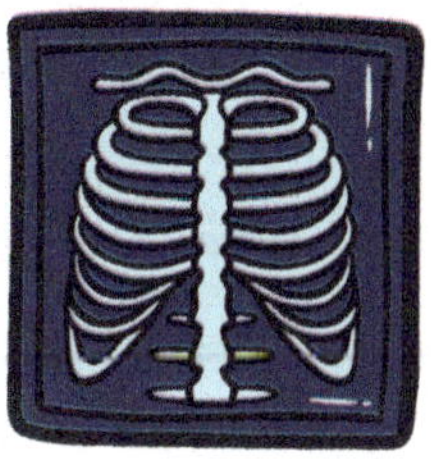

x-ray

Write the letter X

X X X X

X

X

X

Now continue in your red and blue lined exercise book

Fun Fact: Did you know x-rays are used to photograph old objects like artifacts and paintings because it is able to see details that have been lost by time and corrosion.

Comments: ______________________

Date: ____/____/____ Signature: ______________

Follow the directions of the arrows by the numbers starting from the number 1

step 1	step 2	step 3: complete
1 →	1 → 2 ↙	3 →

Z 
zebra crossing

Write the letter Z

Z Z Z Z

Z

Z

Z

Now continue in your red and blue lined exercise book

Safety - Cross with safety. Look for the zebra crossing before you cross the street. Research the words zebra crossing to see how it got its name.

Comments: ______

Date: ___/___/___ Signature: ______

anti-clockwise, curved & straight

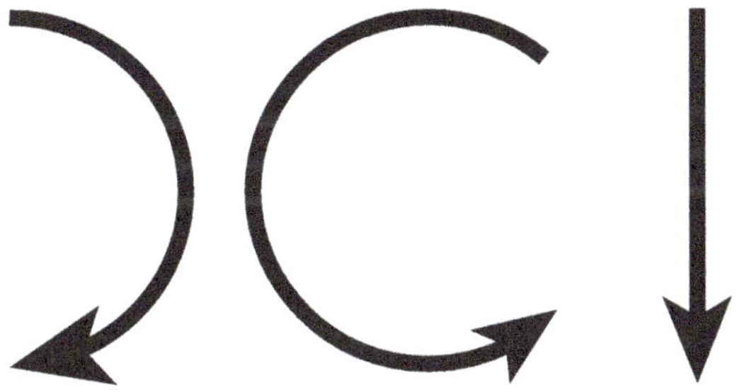

c a q g d

Follow the directions of the arrows by the numbers starting from the number 1

step 1

c 1

step 2

c 2

step 3: complete

c 3

c 

castle

Write the letter c

c c c c

c

c

c

Now continue in your red and blue lined exercise book

Do you know there is a castle around the Savannah in Trinidad? It is called the Stollmeyer's Castle which is one of the seven magnificent buildings. Ask your parent or guardian to take you there to see the castle.

Comments: ____________________

Date: ____/____/____ Signature: ____________________

Follow the directions of the arrows by the numbers starting from the number 1

step 1

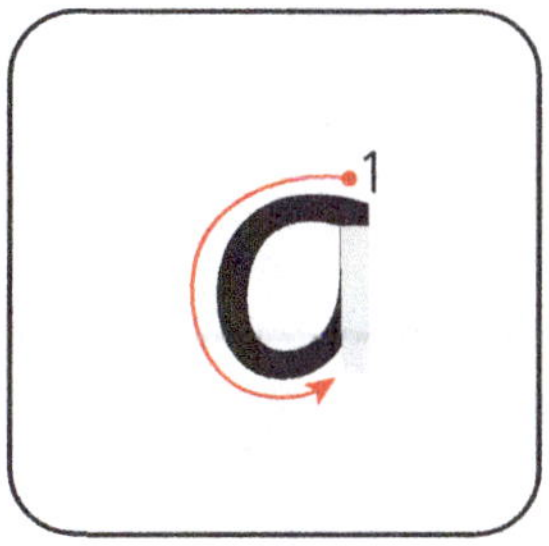

step 2

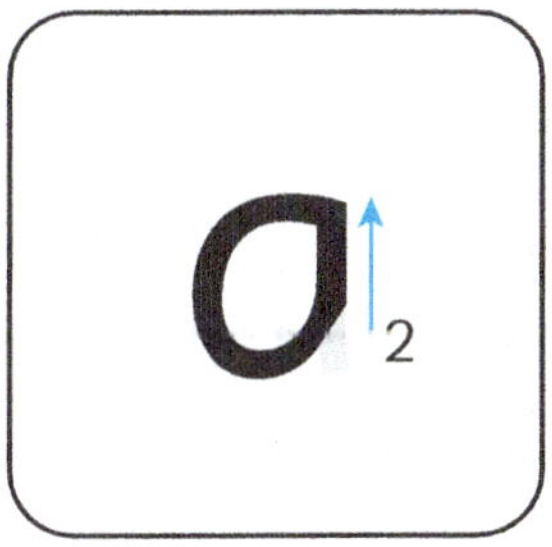

step 3: complete

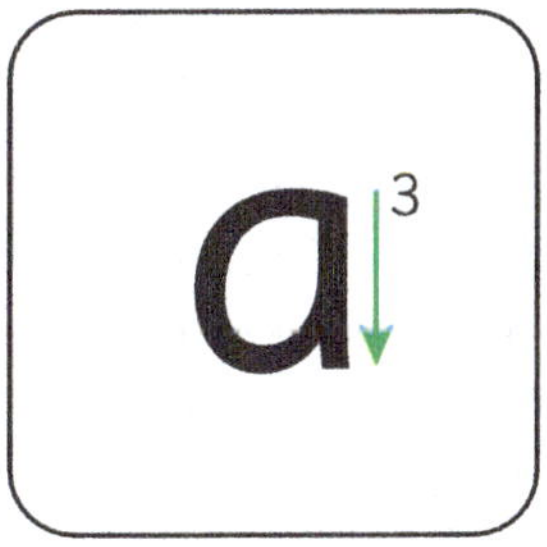

a

ants

Write the letter a

a a a a

a

a

a

Now continue in your red and blue lined exercise book

Fun Fact: The bullet ant is said to have the most powerful sting in the world. Do a bit more research about ants.

Comments: ______________________________

Date: ____/____/______ Signature: ______________________

Follow the directions of the arrows by the numbers starting from the number 1

step 1

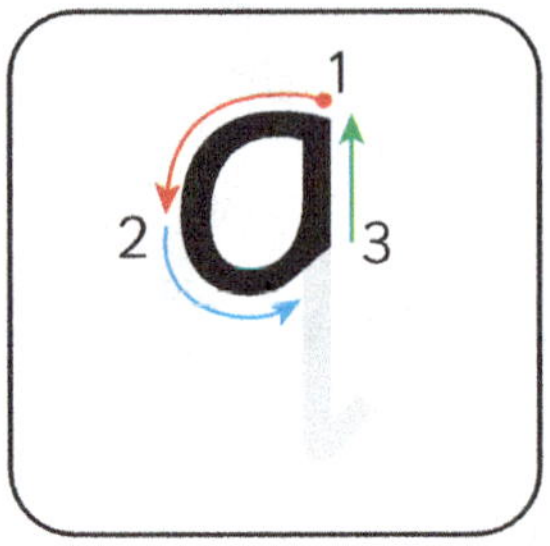

step 2

step 3: complete

Write the letter q

Now continue in your red and blue lined exercise book

I wonder what she is thinking about? She probably has a question to ask. Play a guessing game with a friend or family member, see if the person can guess what you are thinking about.

Comments: ______________________

Date: ___ / ___ / ___ Signature: ______________________

Follow the directions of the arrows by the numbers starting from the number 1

step 1 step 2 step 3: complete

g

gate

Write the letter g

g g g g

g

g

g

Now continue in your red and blue lined exercise book

Safety: For safety - remember to close the gate at all times.

Comments:

Date: / /

Signature:

Follow the directions of the arrows by the numbers starting from the number 1

step 1

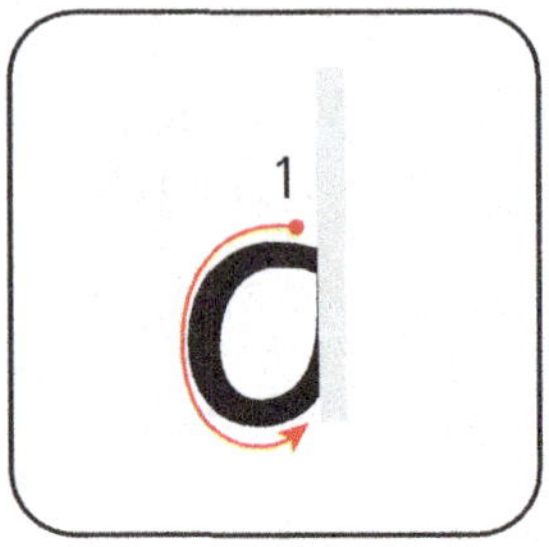

step 2

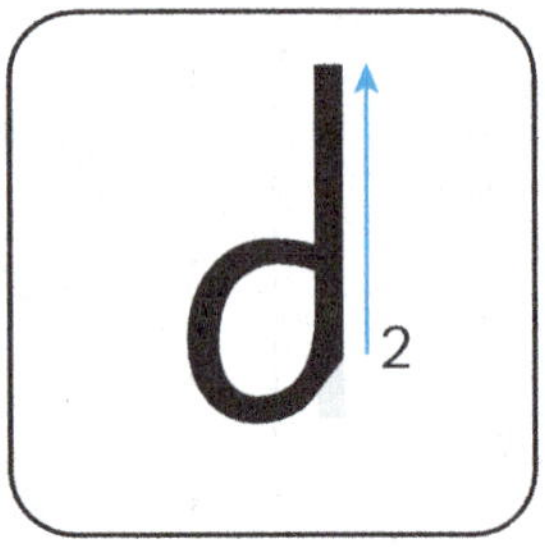

step 3: complete

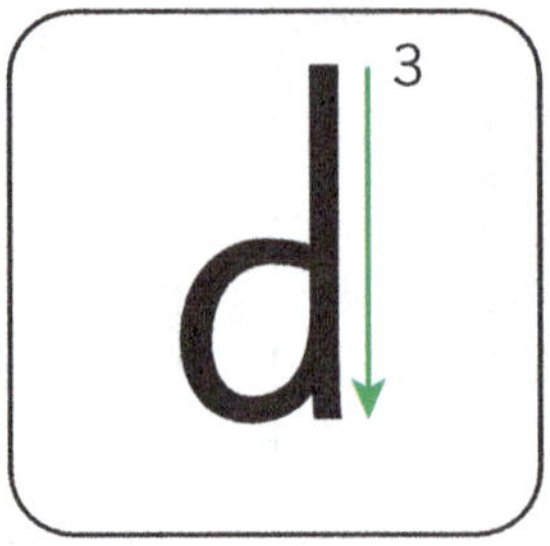

d

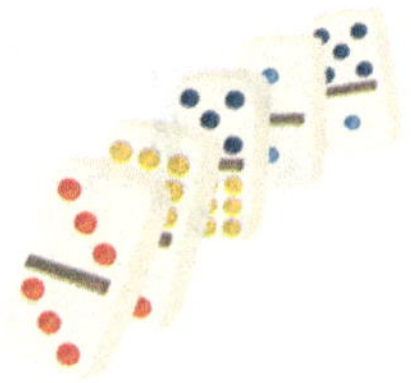

dominoes

Write the letter d

d d d d

d

d

d

Now continue in your red and blue lined exercise book

Fun fact: Did you know that the dots on dominoes are called pips? Do a bit more research and play the game during the week when time allows. Stick this page up in a creative corner in your room.

Comments: ______________________

Date: ____/____/____ Signature: ______________

straight, curved & clockwise

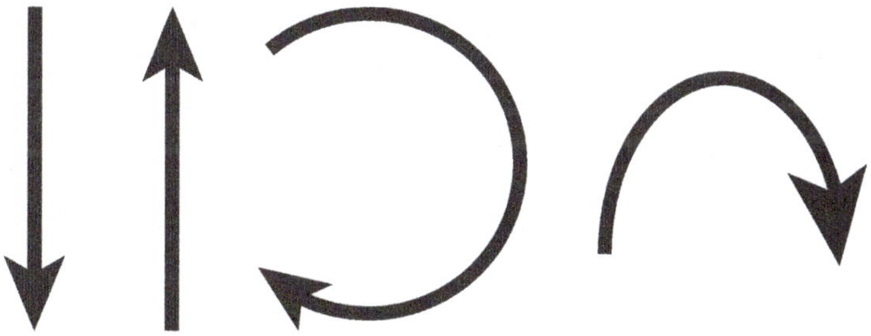

r n h m b

Follow the directions of the arrows by the numbers starting from the number 1

step 1

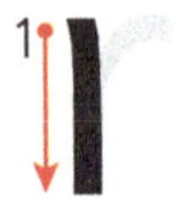

step 2

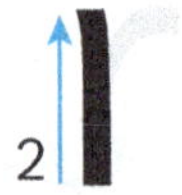

step 3: complete

r 

rainbow

Write the letter r

r r r r

r

r

r

Now continue in your red and blue lined exercise book

Draw and colour the rainbow and add something interesting to the end of the rainbow. Now stick it up in a creative corner in school or in your room. Research: Why does a rainbow appear in the sky?

Comments: ____________________

Date: ____ / ____ / ____ Signature: ____________________

Follow the directions of the arrows by the numbers starting from the number 1

step 1

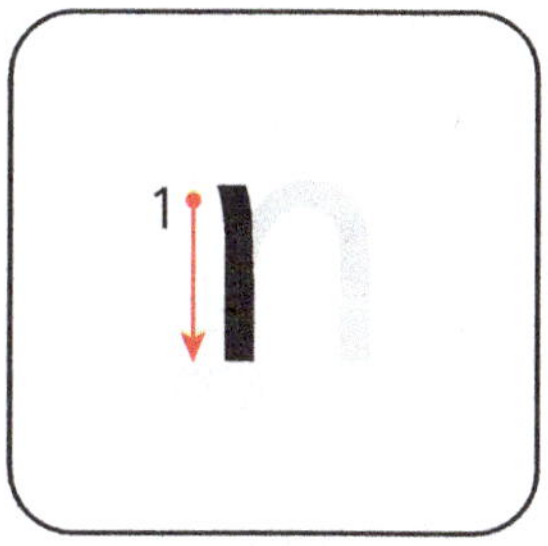

step 2

step 3: complete

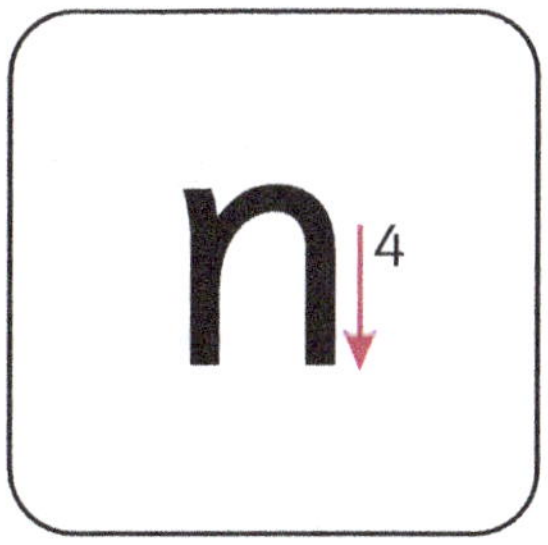

n

net

Write the letter n

n n n n

n

n

n

Now continue in your red and blue lined exercise book

Do you know that there are four main types of fishing nets. One is called a Seine, it is used to catch sardines, herring, tuna and other fish.

Comments:

Date: / /

Signature:

Follow the directions of the arrows by the numbers starting from the number 1

step 1	step 2	step 3: complete	
1 l	3 2 h	h 4	h house

Write the letter h

h h h h

h

h

h

Now continue in your red and blue lined exercise book

There are different types of houses: townhouse, apartment and much more. Draw the type of house you would like to live in.

Comments:

Date: / /

Signature:

Follow the directions of the arrows by the numbers starting from the number 1

step 1

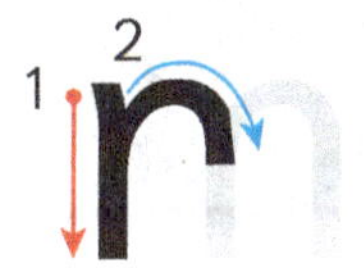

step 2

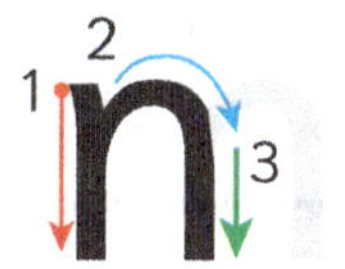

step 3: complete

m

map

Write the letter m

m m m m

m

m

m

Now continue in your red and blue lined exercise book

This is a map of Trinidad and Tobago. Explore the map to see what area you live. Look at other areas you would like to journey to. Do this activity for your country.

Comments: ____________________

Date: ____ / ____ / ____ Signature: ____________________

Follow the directions of the arrows by the numbers starting from the number 1

step 1 | step 2 | step 3: complete

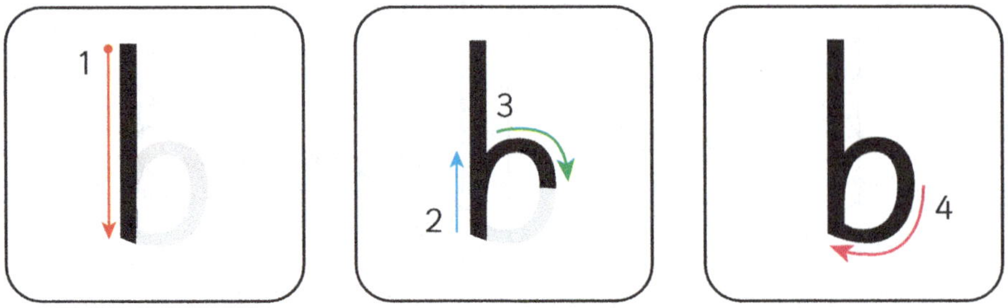

b

ball

Write the letter b

b b b b

b

b

b

Now continue in your red and blue lined exercise book

Cricket is a sport that uses a bat and a ball. It is played in Trinidad as well as other countries. Did you know that Brian Lara has a lot of world records in cricket? Do some research about cricket and try to play it on the weekend.

Comments: ____________________

Date: ___/___/___ Signature: ____________________

odd & different lines

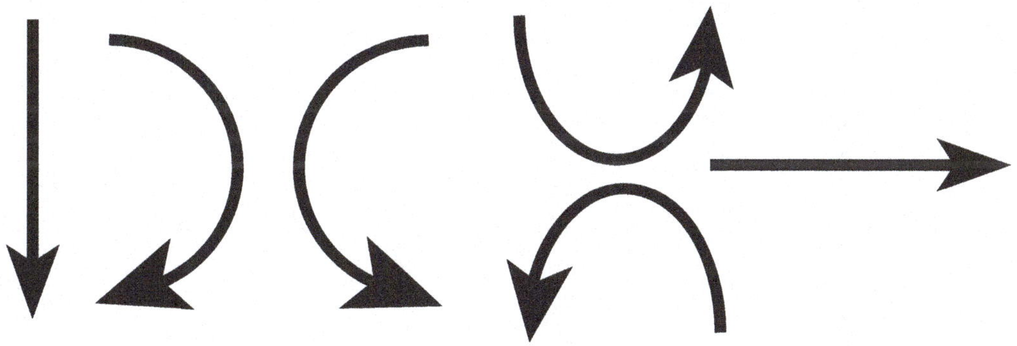

s f u y

Follow the directions of the arrows by the numbers starting from the number 1

step 1 | step 2 | step 3: complete

S
salamander

Write the letter S

S S S S

S

S

S

Now continue in your red and blue lined exercise book

Do you know that a salamander's skin is poisonous? Wash your hands properly after touching a salamander.

Comments: ____________________

Date: ___/___/___ Signature: ____________________

Follow the directions of the arrows by the numbers starting from the number 1

step 1	step 2	step 3: complete
1	2	3 f

f 

flag

Write the letter f

f f f f

f

f

f

Now continue in your red and blue lined exercise book

This is the National flag of Trinidad and Tobago, recall some of the places you have seen it. See how many other flags you can learn about.

Comments: ______________________

Date: ____/____/____ Signature: ______________________

Follow the directions of the arrows by the numbers starting from the number 1

step 1	step 2	step 3: complete
1 u	2 u 3	u 4

u underwater

Write the letter u

u u u u

u

u

u

Now continue in your red and blue lined exercise book

The stingray is an animal that lives underwater. What are some other creatures live underwater?

Comments:

Date: / / Signature:

Follow the directions of the arrows by the numbers starting from the number 1

step 1

step 2

step 3: complete

y  yoga

Write the letter y

y

y

y

y

Now continue in your red and blue lined exercise book

Healthy Lifestyle: Do some yoga exercises today. What else can you do to exercise?

Comments: ______________________

Date: ____/____/____ Signature: ______________

stand alone

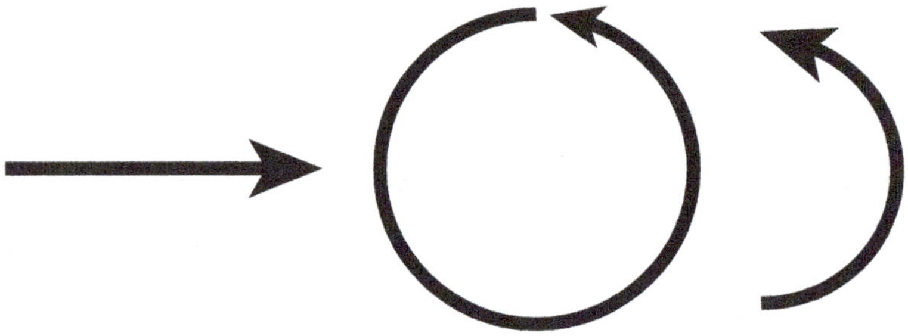

o e

Follow the directions of the arrows by the numbers starting from the number 1

step 1

1

step 2

1
2

step 3: complete

o 3

o 
otter

Write the letter O

o o o o

o

o

o

Now continue in your red and blue lined exercise book

Fun fact: Did you know that sea otters have the thickest fur of any animal?

Comments:

Date: / /

Signature:

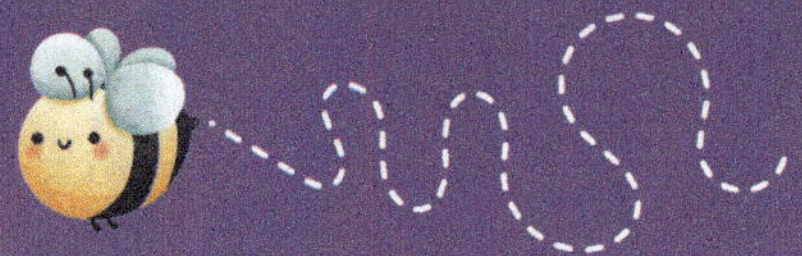

Follow the directions of the arrows by the numbers starting from the number 1

step 1

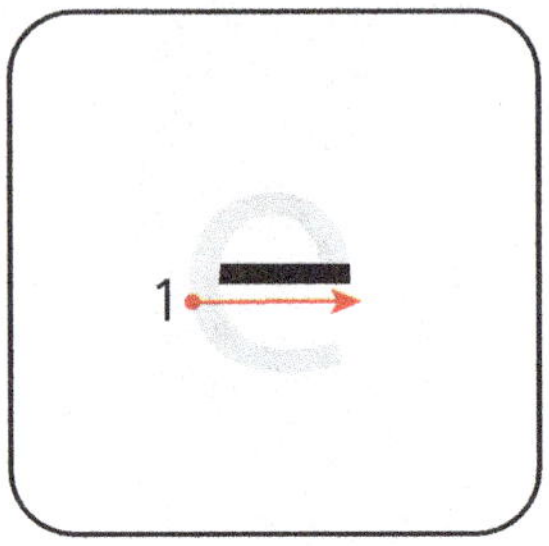

step 2

step 3: complete

e

eggs

Write the letter e

e e e e

e

e

e

Now continue in your red and blue lined exercise book

Eggs can be fried, scrambled and poached to be eaten. Research on more ways eggs can be prepared, as well as its health benefits.

Comments: ______________________

Date: ___/___/___ Signature: ______________________

Uppercase Letters

A B C D E F G H
I J K L M N O P Q
R S T U V W X Y Z

UPPERCASE LETTER FORMATION GROUPED

STRAIGHT & ACROSS

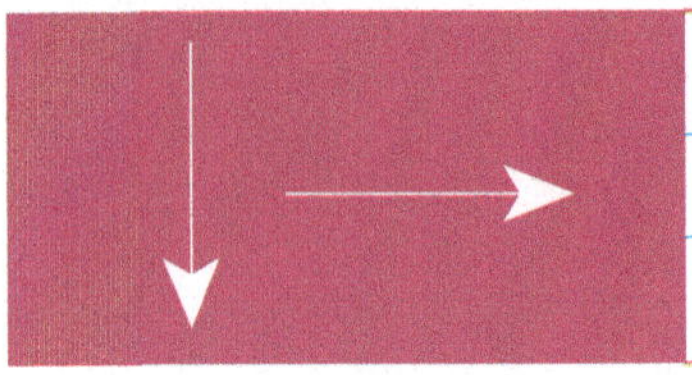

TILHFE

SLANTED, STRAIGHT & ACROSS

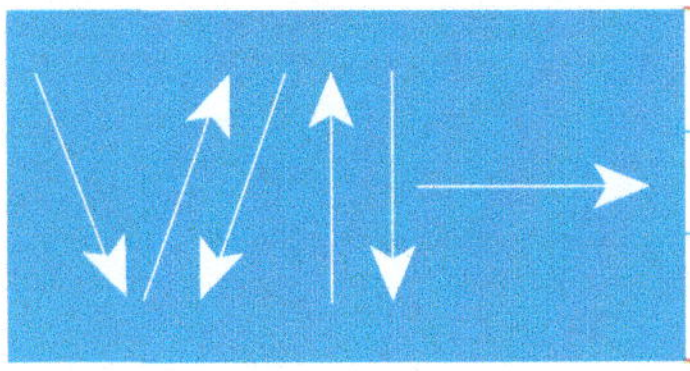

VWYXZKANM

ANTI-CLOCKWISE & STRAIGHT

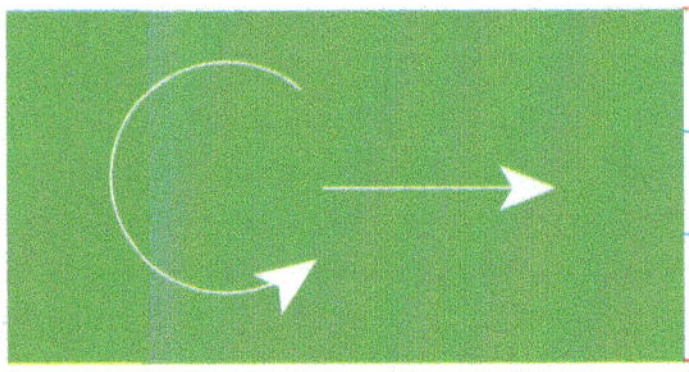

CG

STRAIGHT, CLOCKWISE & SLANTED

PRBD

ODD-DIFFERENT LINES

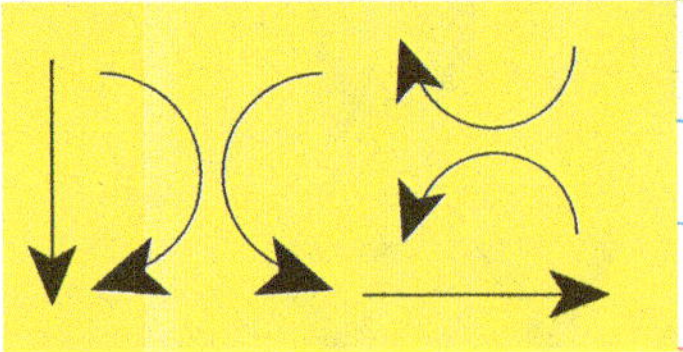

SUJ

STAND ALONE, ROUNDED & SLANTED

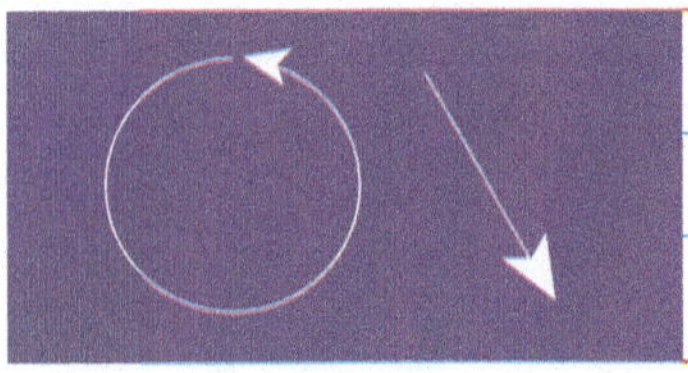

OQ

Sample Page

All the letters should be completed like this in three rows for all the activities.

Follow the directions of the arrows by the numbers starting from the number 1

step 1 | step 2 | step 3: complete

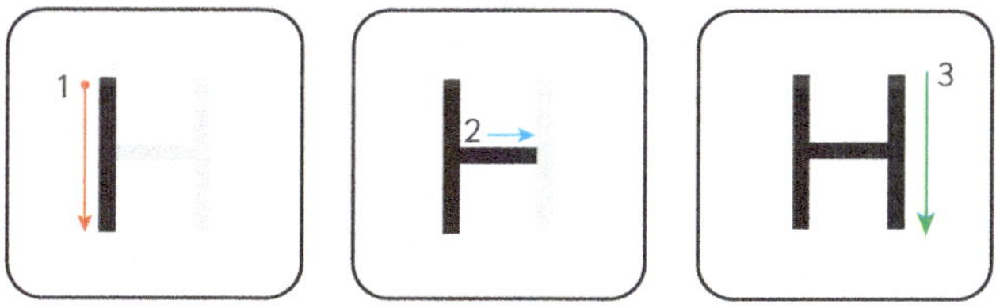

H HEDGEHOG

Write the letter H

Now continue in your red and blue lined exercise book

Fun Fact: Did you know that HEDGEHOGS love to explore mazes and tunnels? Do a HEDGEHOG craft this week.

Comments: ______________________

Date: ___/___/___ Signature: ______________

STRAIGHT & ACROSS

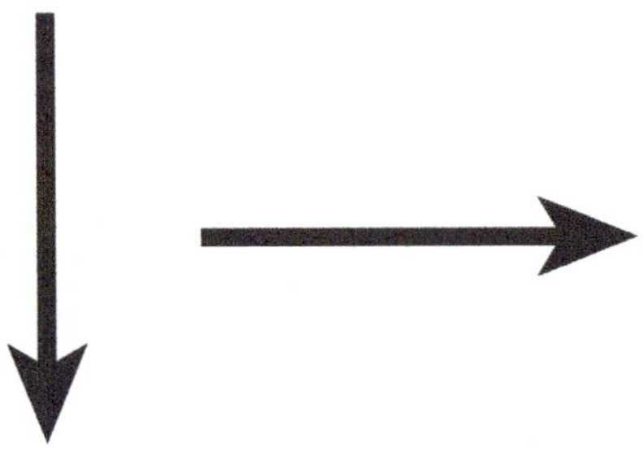

T I L H F E

Follow the directions of the arrows by the numbers starting from the number 1

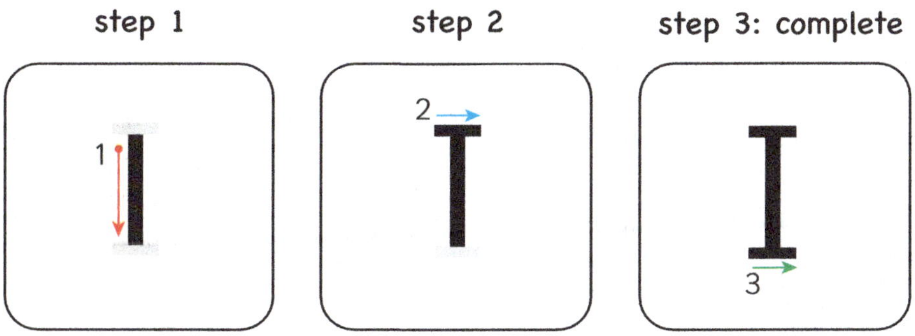

Write the letter I

Now continue in your red and blue lined exercise book

Fun fact: Did you know that IGUANAS can detach their tail if caught and grow another one? Also, IGUANAS eat leaves and fruits. Research to find out what else IGUANAS eat. Make an iguana out of playdoh.

Comments: ______________________

Date: ____/____/____ Signature: ______________________

Follow the directions of the arrows by the numbers starting from the number 1

step 1

1 L

step 2

L 2

step 3: complete

L

L 

LOCK

Write the letter L

L L L L

L

L

L

Now continue in your red and blue lined exercise book

LOCKS are used to secure things. However, do not close a LOCK unless the key is visible to you.

Comments: ______

Date: ___/___/___ Signature: ______

Follow the directions of the arrows by the numbers starting from the number 1

step 1	step 2	step 3: complete	
1 H	2 H	H 3	H HEDGEHOG

Write the letter H

H H H H

H

H

H

Now continue in your red and blue lined exercise book

Fun Fact: Did you know that HEDGEHOGS love to explore mazes and tunnels? Do a HEDGEHOG craft this week.

Comments:

Date: / / Signature:

Follow the directions of the arrows by the numbers starting from the number 1

step 1 | step 2 | step 3: complete

1 T

2 T

T

T 

TURKEY

Write the letter T

T T T T

T

T

T

Now continue in your red and blue lined exercise book

Did you know that TURKEYS lay one clutch of eggs per year.
This means they lay one egg each day until their clutch is finished.
Make a TURKEY sandwich for lunch tomorrow.

Comments: ____________________

Date: ___/___/___ Signature: ____________________

Follow the directions of the arrows by the numbers starting from the number 1

step 1 — 1

step 2 — 2

step 3: complete — 3

F 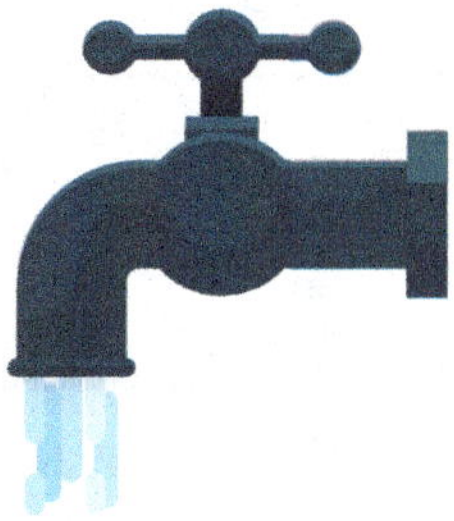

FAUCET

Write the letter F

F F F F

F

F

F

Now continue in your red and blue lined exercise book

Please remember to turn off the FAUCET to conserve (save) water.

Comments: ______________________

Date: ___/___/___ Signature: ______________________

Follow the directions of the arrows by the numbers starting from the number 1

step 1

1 I

step 2

2 F 3

step 3: complete

E 4

E 

ECHINDA

Write the letter E

E E E E

E

E

E

Now continue in your red and blue lined exercise book

Fun fact: Did you know the baby ECHIDNA stays in the mother's pouch for seven (7) weeks. Research more about it today. Stick this picture up in your room when completed.

Comments: ______

Date: __/__/__ Signature: ______

SLANTED, STRAIGHT & ACROSS

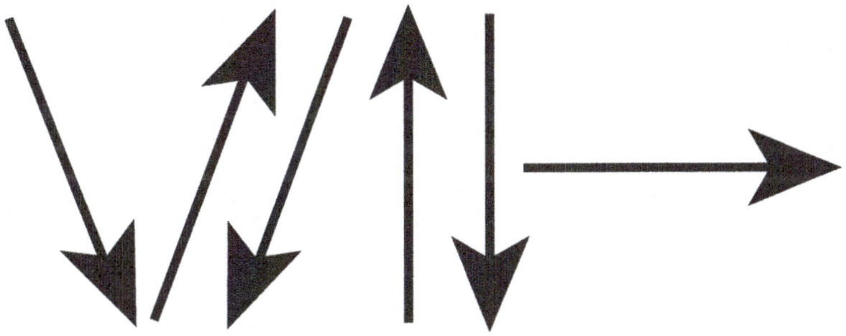

V W Y X Z

K A N M

Follow the directions of the arrows by the numbers starting from the number 1

step 1	step 2	step 3: complete
1 V	V 2	V

V 

VACUUM

Write the letter V

V V V V

V

V

V

Now continue in your red and blue lined exercise book

VACUUMS are very useful to pick up dust particles. Help your parents or guardians VACUUM this week.

Comments: ____________________

Date: ___/___/___ Signature: ____________________

Follow the directions of the arrows by the numbers starting from the number 1

step 1 step 2 step 3: complete

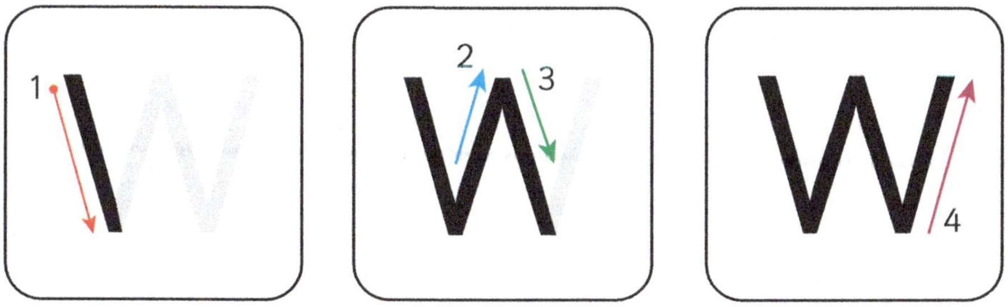

W 

WELL

Write the letter W

W W W

W

W

W

Now continue in your red and blue lined exercise book

The average lifespan of a water WELL is between 30 to 50 years. Craft time: make a water WELL with a tissue roll and other craft resources.

Comments:

Date: / / Signature:

Follow the directions of the arrows by the numbers starting from the number 1

step 1 | step 2 | step 3: complete

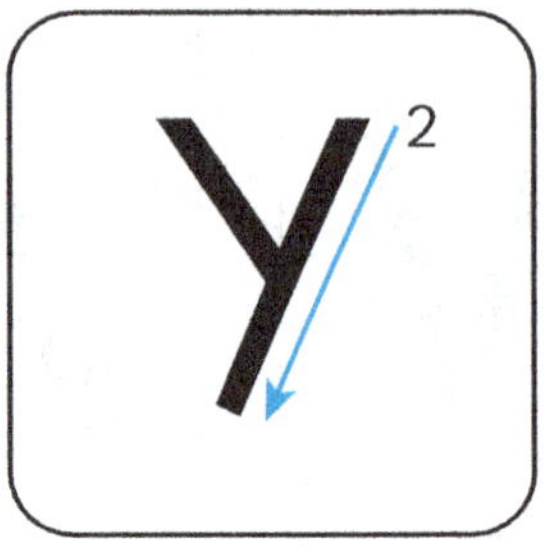

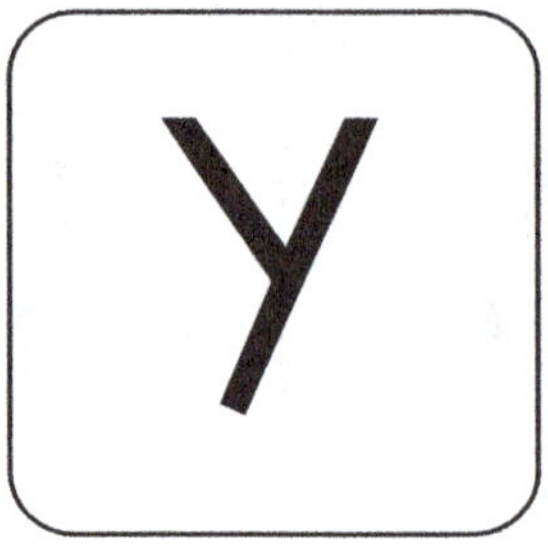

Write the letter y

y y y w

y

y

y

Now continue in your red and blue lined exercise book

YOGURT aids in digestion. Try a different YOGURT flavour today!

Comments: ______________________

Date: ____/____/____ Signature: ______________________

Follow the directions of the arrows by the numbers starting from the number 1

step 1	step 2	step 3: complete
1 \	X 2	X

X

XIPHIAS
SWORDFISH

Write the letter X

X X X X

X

X

X

Now continue in your red and blue lined exercise book

Fun Fact: Do you know that SWORDFISHES lose all their teeth and scales by adulthood? Make a SWORDFISH out of playdoh or paper.

Comments: ______________________

Date: ___/___/___ Signature: ______________________

Follow the directions of the arrows by the numbers starting from the number 1

step 1

1 Z

step 2

Z 2

step 3: complete

Z 3

Z

ZOOKEEPER

Write the letter Z

Z Z Z Z

Z

Z

Z

Now continue in your red and blue lined exercise book

This is a ZOOKEEPER, he takes care of animals. What would you like to be when you grow up?

Comments: ______________________________

Date: ____/____/____ Signature: ______________________

Follow the directions of the arrows by the numbers starting from the number 1

step 1

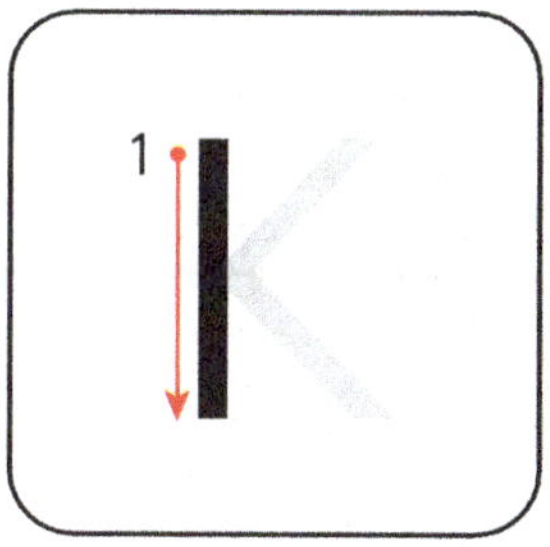

step 2

step 3: complete

K

KOALA

Write the letter K

K K K K

K

K

K

Now continue in your red and blue lined exercise book

Fun Fact: Do you know KOALAS can sleep up to 18 hours a day.
Explore more facts about KOALAS.

Comments: ____________________

Date: ____/____/____ Signature: ____________________

Follow the directions of the arrows by the numbers starting from the number 1

step 1

1 A

step 2

2 A

step 3: complete

3 A

A 

AVOCADO

Write the letter A

A A A A

A

A

A

Now continue in your red and blue lined exercise book

AVOCADOS improve your overall skin health. Ask your parents or guardians to purchase an AVOCADO and taste it.

Comments:

Date: / /

Signature:

Follow the directions of the arrows by the numbers starting from the number 1

step 1: 1 N

step 2: 2 N

step 3: complete: N 3

N

NOODLES

Write the letter N

N N N N

N

N

N

Now continue in your red and blue lined exercise book

Fun Fact: Did you know Ramen NOODLES was invented in Japan? Dine out this weekend or make a meal at home using NOODLES.

Comments: ______

Date: __/__/__ Signature: ______

Follow the directions of the arrows by the numbers starting from the number 1

step 1

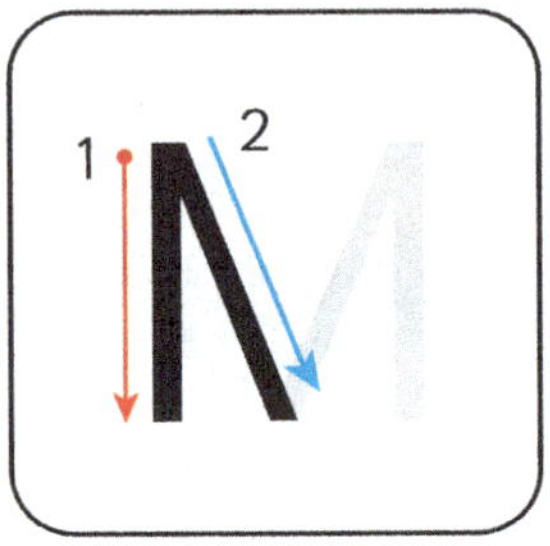

step 2

step 3: complete

M 

MANDARINS

Write the letter M

M M M M

M

M

M

Now continue in your red and blue lined exercise book

Healthy Lifestyle: Make a fruit salad using MANDARINS. Plant the seeds to continue replenishing the forest.

Comments: ____________________

Date: ___/___/___ Signature: ____________________

ANTI-CLOCKWISE & STRAIGHT

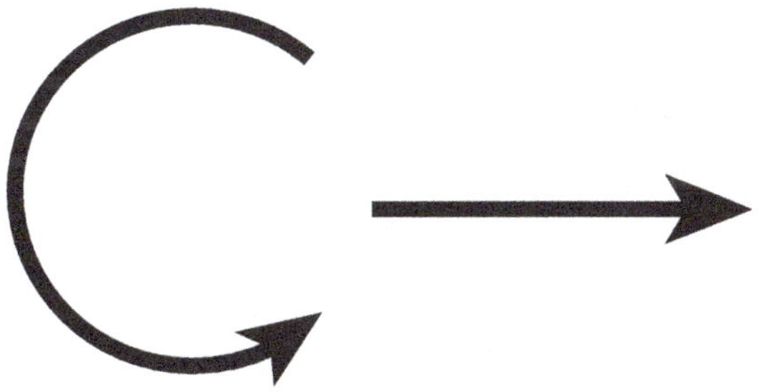

C G

Follow the directions of the arrows by the numbers starting from the number 1

step 1 | step 2 | step 3: complete

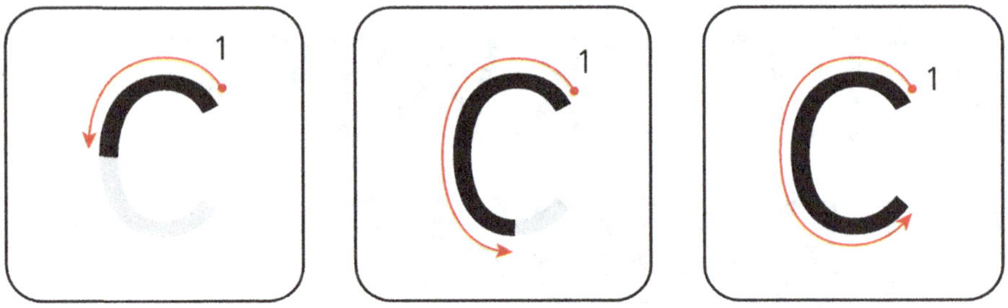

C

CAKE

Write the letter C

C C C C

C

C

C

Now continue in your red and blue lined exercise book

This is a three (3) layered CAKE. Bake a CAKE with your parents or guardians this weekend. Create fun memories: stick this page in your room in the creative corner.

Comments: ______________________

Date: ___/___/___ Signature: ______________________

Follow the directions of the arrows by the numbers starting from the number 1

step 1 | step 2 | step 3: complete

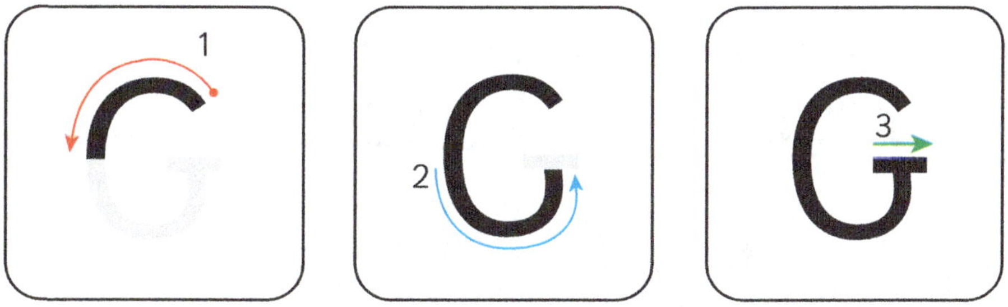

Write the letter G

G G G G
G
G
G

Now continue in your red and blue lined exercise book

Did you know GORILLAS have 16 types of call? For example, they make short bark sounds when they are alarmed or curious. Research the other 15 calls.

Comments: ____________________

Date: ___/___/___ Signature: ____________________

STRAIGHT & CLOCKWISE

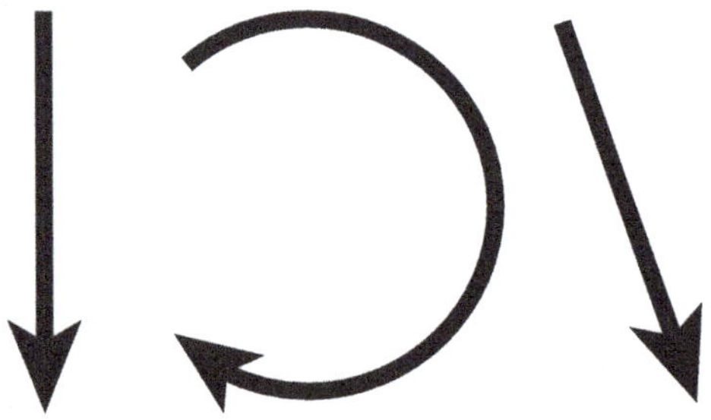

P R B D

Follow the directions of the arrows by the numbers starting from the number 1

step 1 | step 2 | step 3: complete

P 

POPCORN

Write the letter P

P P P P

P

P

P

Now continue in your red and blue lined exercise book

Have a POPCORN night while watching a movie this weekend.

Comments: ____________________

Date: ___/___/___ Signature: ____________________

Follow the directions of the arrows by the numbers starting from the number 1

step 1 | step 2 | step 3: complete

RASPBERRY

Write the letter R

R R R R

R

R

R

Now continue in your red and blue lined exercise book

Try some RASPBERRY flavoured yogurt filled RASPBERRIES! Yum! Yum!

Comments: ______________________________

Date: ____ / ____ / ____ Signature: ______________________

Follow the directions of the arrows by the numbers starting from the number 1

step 1 | step 2 | step 3: complete

1 B | 2 P | 3 B

B 

BINS

Write the letter B

B B B B

B

B

B

Now continue in your red and blue lined exercise book

Remember to save our planet - Reduce, Reuse and Recycle. (3 R's). Look for the specially marked BINS in your neighbourhood or city.

Comments:

Date: / / Signature:

Follow the directions of the arrows by the numbers starting from the number 1

step 1 — 1 D

step 2 — 2 D

step 3: complete — D 2

D 

DESERT

Write the letter D

D D D D

D

D

D

Now continue in your red and blue lined exercise book

Fun Fact: A lot of animals that live in the DESERT are nocturnal (active at night). Make a DESERT diorama.

Comments: ______________________

Date: ____ / ____ / ____ Signature: ______________________

ODD-DIFFERENT LINES

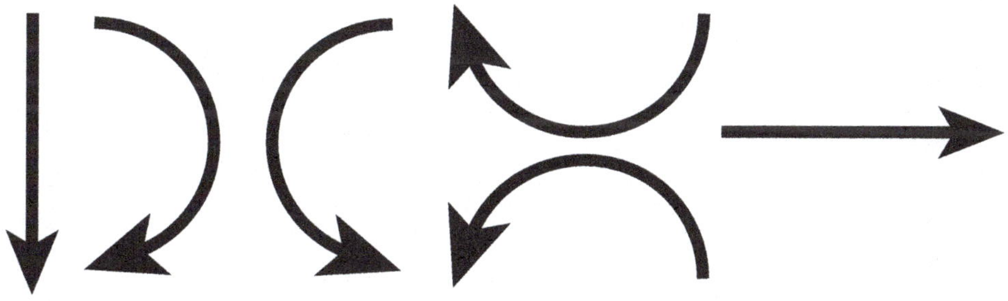

S U J

Follow the directions of the arrows by the numbers starting from the number 1

step 1

step 2

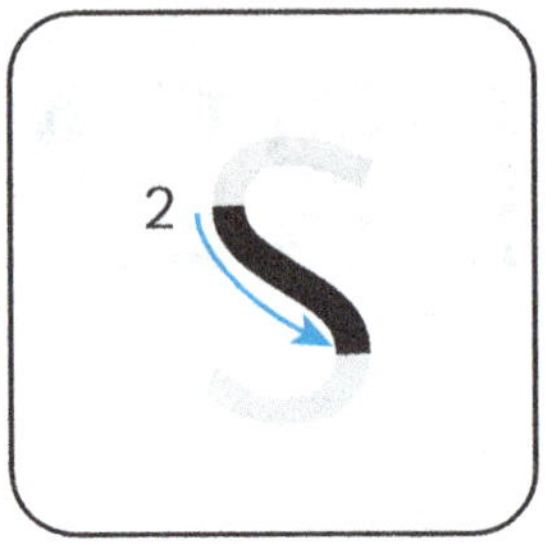

step 3: complete

S

SPACE

Write the letter S

S S S S

S

S

S

Now continue in your red and blue lined exercise book

Fun Fact: Did you know that a full NASA SPACE suit costs approximately $12,000,000 US? Draw a picture of an astronaut in SPACE and colour or paint it, then stick it up in your room.

Comments: ______________________________

Date: ____/____/____ Signature: ______________________

Follow the directions of the arrows by the numbers starting from the number 1

step 1 | step 2 | step 3: complete

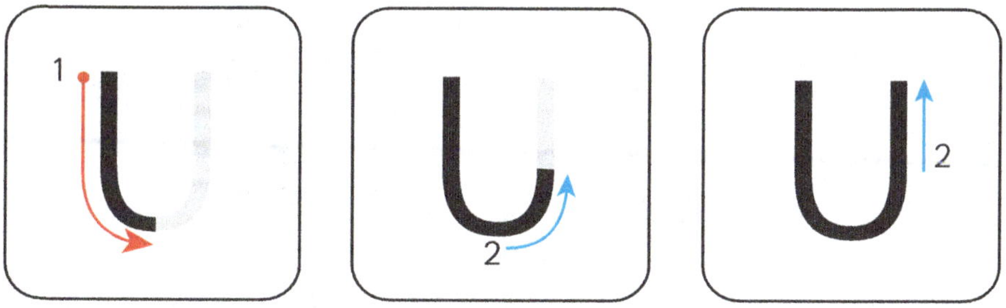

U

UNHAPPY

Write the letter U

U U U U
U
U
U

Now continue in your red and blue lined exercise book

Let's talk about emotions: Why do you think she is UNHAPPY? Reflect on something that made you UNHAPPY. Now let's explore something that made you happy. Think of other emotions and facial expressions, now play a facial expressions game.

Comments: ____________________

Date: ___/___/___ Signature: ____________________

Follow the directions of the arrows by the numbers starting from the number 1

step 1 — 1 J

step 2 — J 2

step 3: complete — 3 J

J 

JETSKI

Write the letter J

J J J J

J

J

J

Now continue in your red and blue lined exercise book

Fun Fact: Did you know that Clayton Jacobson II, invented the JETSKI?
The first protype was made in 1965.

Comments: ____________________

Date: ____/____/____ Signature: ____________________

STAND ALONE-
ROUNDED &
SLANTED

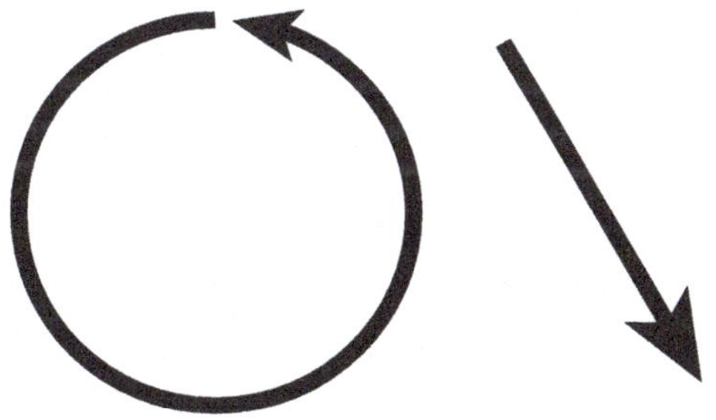

O Q

Follow the directions of the arrows by the numbers starting from the number 1

step 1	step 2	step 3: complete	
1 (	O 2	O	O

OYSTER

Write the letter O

O O O O

O

O

O

Now continue in your red and blue lined exercise book

Fun Fact: Do you know OYSTERS can filter 1.3 gallons of water per hour.
Now you know! Do some more research to find out some more fun facts.
Activity: make an OYSTER craft.

Comments: ____________________

Date: ___/___/___ Signature: ____________________

Follow the directions of the arrows by the numbers starting from the number 1

step 1

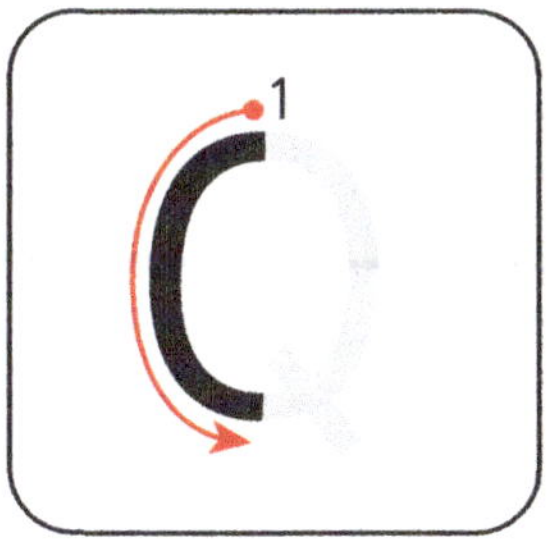

step 2

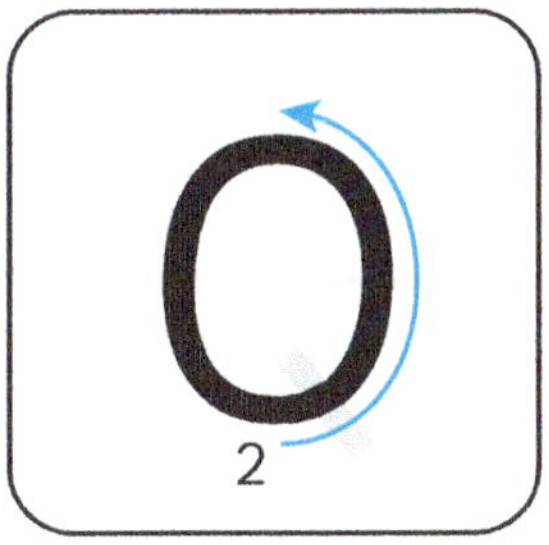

step 3: complete

Write the letter Q

Now continue in your red and blue lined exercise book

Fun Fact: Do you know a baby QUAIL is called a squab or a squeaker. The QUAILS communicate by making a simple coo sound, a loud "whoe-whoe-oh-oh-oh" or sad "ooooooou" sound.

Comments: ______________________________

Date: ___/___/_____ Signature: ______________________

Letters Testing

common letters

write all the common letters from a - z

Comments:

Date: / / Signature:

Letters Testing

CAPITAL LETTERS

Write all the capital letters from A - Z

Comments:

Date: / /   Signature:

Practice Sentences

Let's get writing!

Write the sentence over and over, until you reach to the end of the section.

The boy is fishing in the river.

The children are playing tag.

Please eat all your fruits.

Comments: ______________________

Date: ___/___/___ Signature: ______________________

Write the sentence over and over, until you reach to the end of the section.

Let us go to the park please.

Can I have some mandarins?

Stingrays live in the ocean.

Comments:

Date: / / Signature:

Form your own sentences

Comments:

Date: / / Signature:

Form your own sentences

Comments: ____________________

Date: ___/___/___ Signature: ____________________

Congratulations you've completed all your letters!

To remember your achievement here's a certificate of completion for you. Cut it out, fill in your name and frame it.

AUNTY V'S BOOKS

PENMANSHIP PERFECT!

Certificate of Completion

Beginners Level

YOU'RE A STAR

____

for completing all your letters.

I am proud of you!

______________ date

______________ signature

QUALITY 100% GUARATEED

About the Author

Veronica Carasquero is a devoted and fervid primary school teacher. She has taught at several pre-schools from the young age of seventeen (17) years old. In combination of her pre-school and primary school teaching, she has accumulated over thirty (30) years experience. To date she teaches at a primary school. Her passion has been and continues to be, seeing children excel in the skills of writing (penmanship) and reading. She holds a certificate from "The Jolly Phonics Program" which focuses on the teaching of letter sounds and writing formation, a certificate from The University of the West Indies (U.W.I) "The 101 on Teaching your Child to Write" which also focuses on letter formation by groups. A Diploma in Montessori Teaching (Dip. Mont. Ed.) from the London Montessori Centre (LMC) London, a Bachelors' in Education, (B.Ed.) (Hons) at the University of Trinidad and Tobago (UTT) and a Masters' in Education (M.Ed.) at the University of New Brunswick Canada (UNB).

Made in the USA
Coppell, TX
21 July 2026

84973055R00059